aerobics

roll-ups

leg raises

side bends

aeroboxing

trunk twists

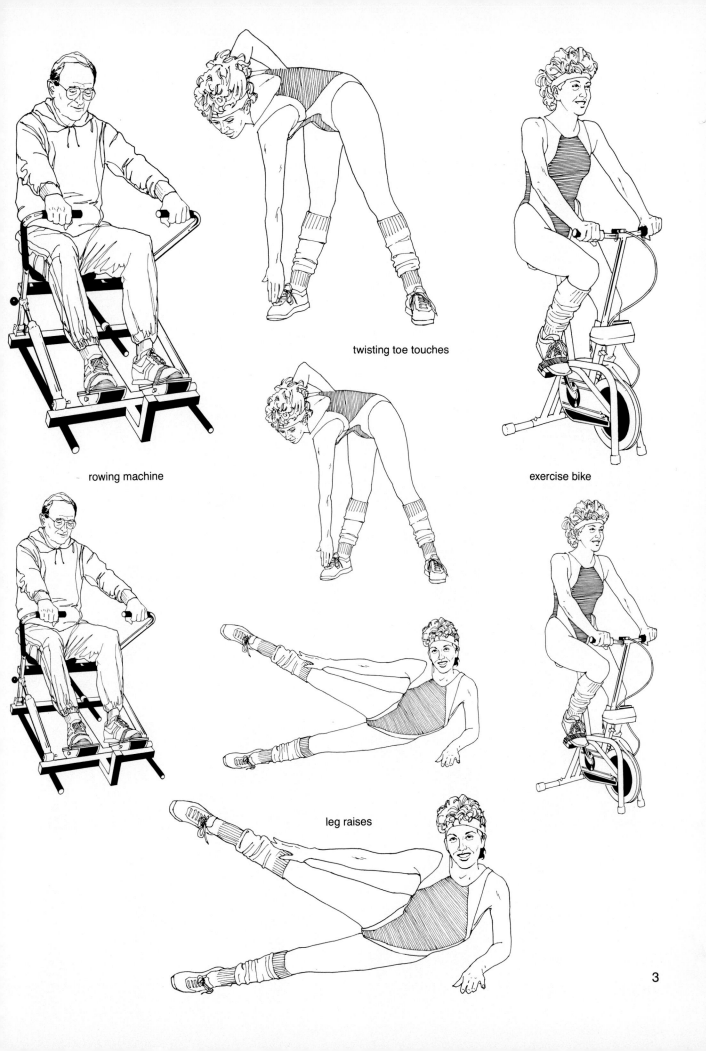

rowing machine

twisting toe touches

exercise bike

leg raises

3

barbell shoulder press

reverse barbell curls

barbell curls

barbell curls

reverse barbell curls

barbell shoulder press

4

alternate dumbbell curls

bench press

barbell curls

barbell and dumbbells

5

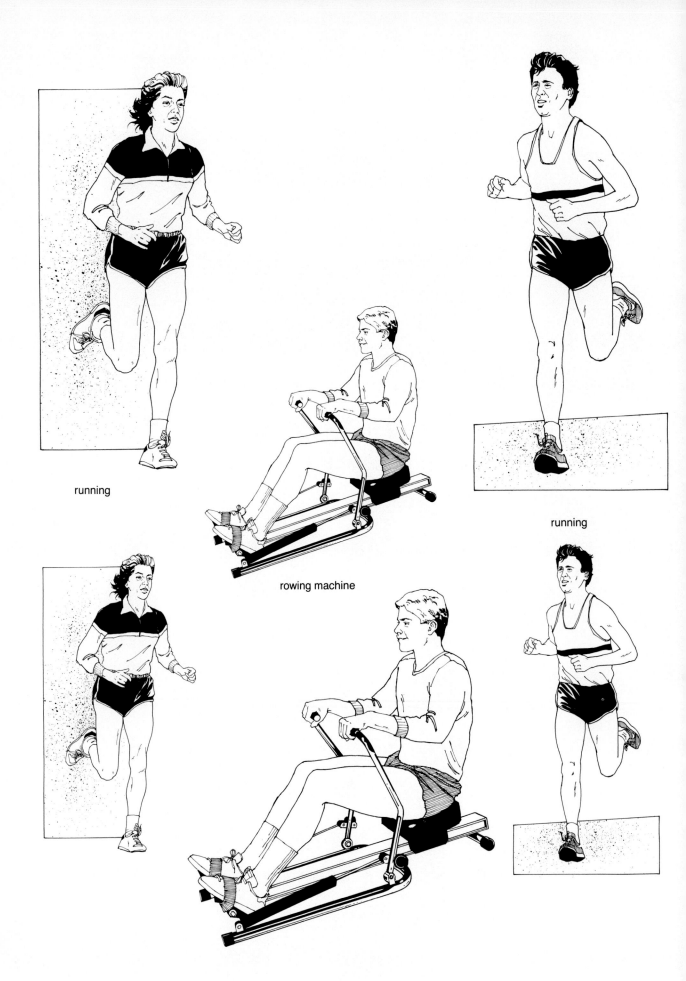

running

running

rowing machine

exercise bike

exercise bike

abdominal and back exerciser

7

exercise bike

exercise bike

abdominal and back exerciser

bench-press machine

exercise bike

lateral-raise machine

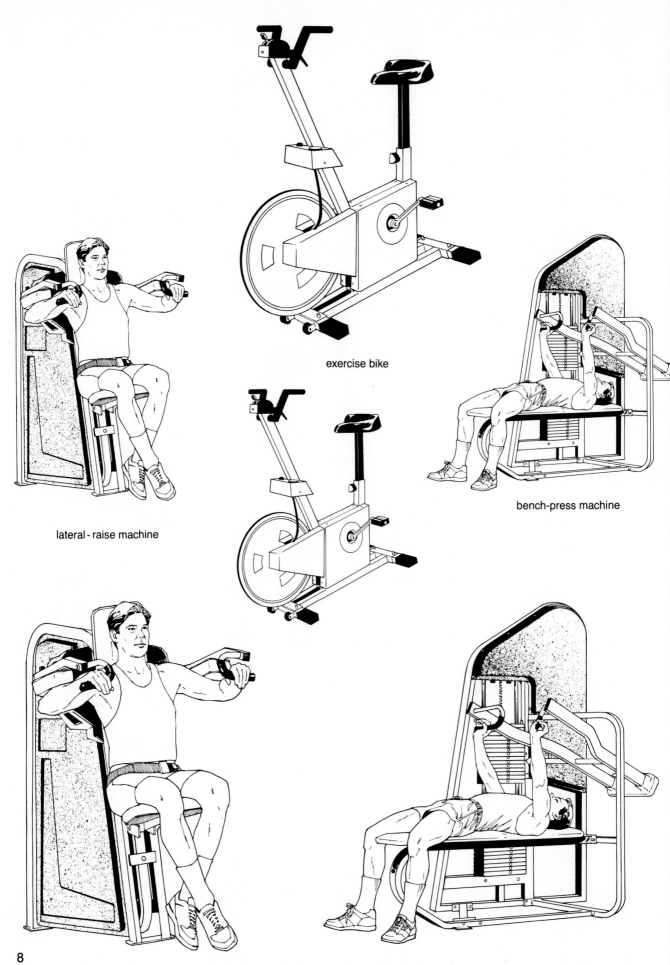

exercise bike

lateral - raise machine

bench-press machine

8

exercise bike

treadmill

ski exerciser

9

dumbbell curls

military press

incline press

shoulder-press machine

alternate dumbbell curls

pull-over machine

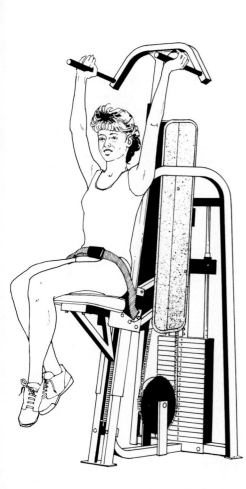

pull-over machine

alternate dumbbell curls

shoulder-press machine

squats

bench press

concentration curls

bench press

bench press

alternate dumbbell curls

warm-down

barbell curls   front raises

warm-down

front raises

barbell curls

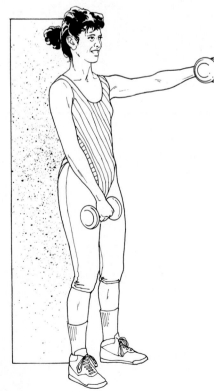

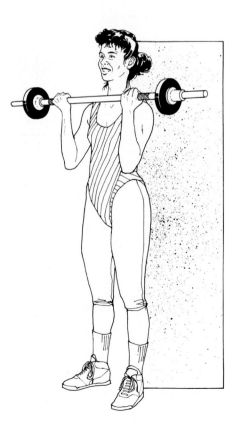

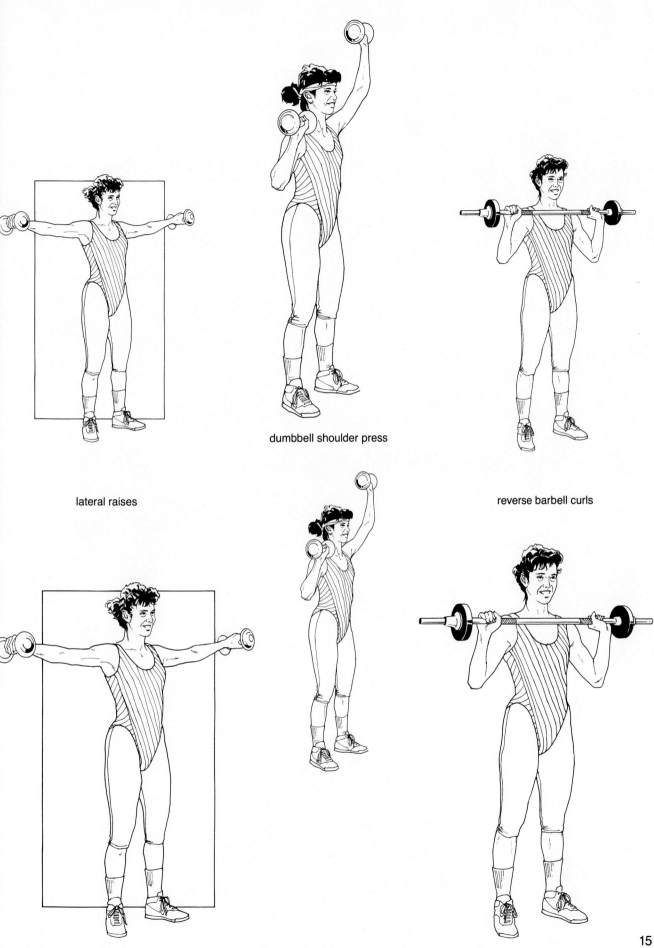

dumbbell shoulder press

lateral raises

reverse barbell curls

dumbbell shoulder press

reverse barbell curls

lateral raises

upright rows

jogging

reverse barbell curls

twisting toe touches

bench press

walking

17

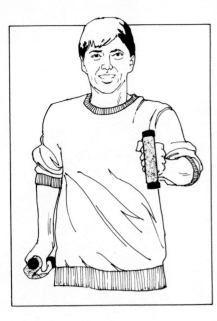

jogging

running

jogging

walking

ski exerciser

jogging

jogging

walking

jogging

running

cycling

jogging

jogging

cycling

cycling

cycling

cycling

cycling

cycling

23

aerobics

aerobics

push-ups

24

jumping rope

jumping rope

jumping rope

sit-ups

aerobics class

push-ups

sit-ups

pull-ups

sit-ups

27

swimming

swimming

swimming

swimming

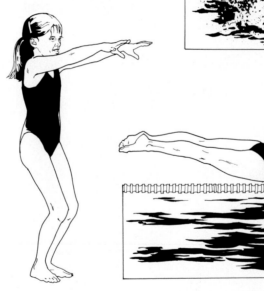

swimming

28

swimming

swimming

swimming

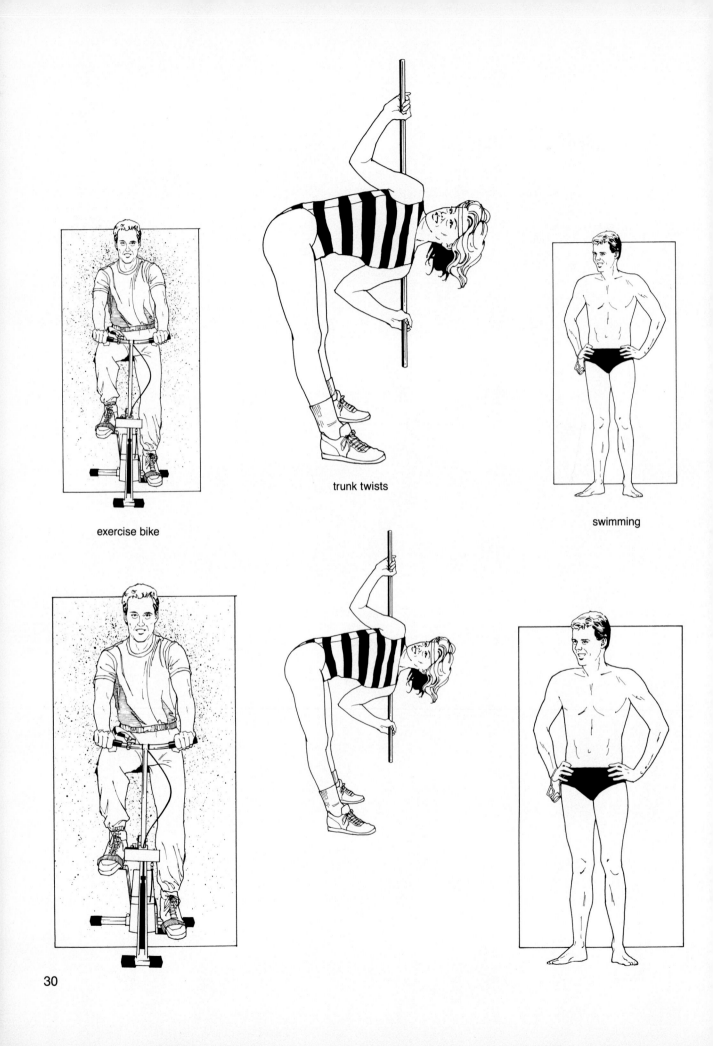

exercise bike

trunk twists

swimming

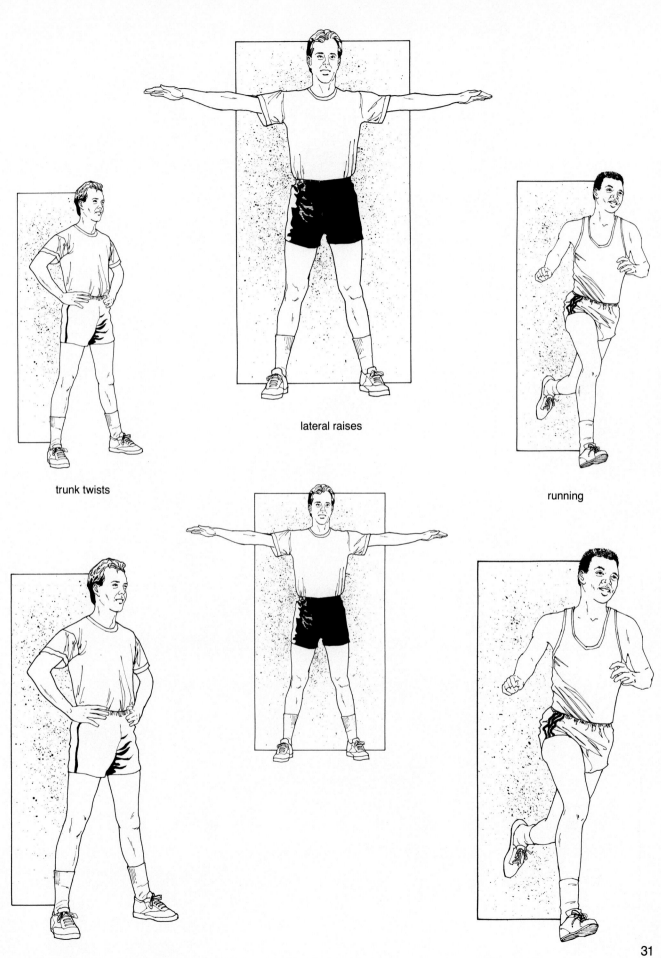

trunk twists

lateral raises

running

31

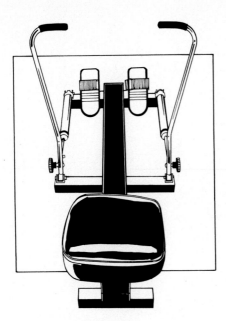

rowing machine

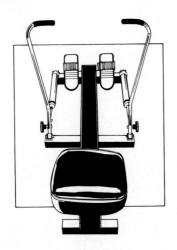

posing

aerobic dumbbells

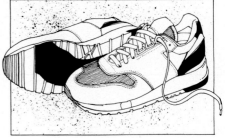

athletic shoes

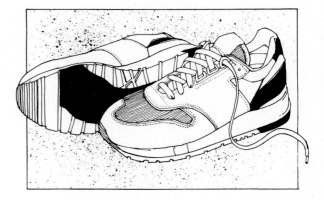